WOMEN Hold Up Half the Sky

*285 Spirited Women and
What They Said About Life,
Love, Work, and Men*

• • •

compiled and edited by
Lee Wilson

PLEASANT VIEW PRESS ■ PLEASANT VIEW, TENNESSEE

Women Hold Up Half The Sky
285 spirited women and what they said about life, love, work, and men

Compiled and edited by Lee Wilson
© 1994 Linda Lee Wilson

Published by Pleasant View Press, P.O. Box 185, Pleasant View, Tennessee 37146. Printed in the United States of America.

To order additional copies of this book, use the order form in the back of the book or write the publisher; quantity discounts are available.

Book design and composition by Bruce Gore / Gore Studio, Inc., Nashville, Tennessee. Text set in Cochin and Stempel Schneidler. Printed by BookCrafters, Chelsea, Michigan.

Library of Congress Catalog Card Number: 93-087504

ISBN: 0-9639815-0-1

This book
is dedicated to women everywhere
who think for themselves and
say what they think.

◆ ◆ ◆

Women hold up half the sky.

NATIVE AMERICAN PROVERB

◆

Every mother is a working mother.

ANONYMOUS

◆

The first time Adam had a chance he laid the blame on women.

NANCY ASTOR (1879–1964)
American-English politician, the first woman elected to the British House of Commons

◆

You don't get to choose how you're going to die. Or when. You can only decide how you're going to live. Now.

JOAN BAEZ (1941–)
American singer and civil rights activist

Happiness is good health and a bad memory.

INGRID BERGMAN (1915–82)
Swedish-American actress

◆

I've been rich and I've been poor; rich is better.

SOPHIE TUCKER (1884–1966)
Russian-American singer

◆

Character contributes to beauty. It fortifies a woman as her youth fades. A mode of conduct, a standard of courage, discipline, fortitude, and integrity can do a great deal to make a woman beautiful.

JACQUELINE BISSET (1946–)
English actress

What is man, when you come to think upon him, but a minutely set, ingenious machine for turning, with infinite artfulness, red wine into urine?

ISAK DINESEN (KAREN BLIXEN: 1885–1962)
Danish writer

◆

I'm just a person trapped inside a woman's body.

ELAYNE BOOSLER (1952–)
American comic

◆

A woman who is loved always has success.

VICKI BAUM (1888–1960)
Austrian-American writer and playwright

Marriage is the deep, deep peace of the double bed after the hurly-burly of the *chaise longue.*

MRS. PATRICK CAMPBELL
(BEATRICE STELLA TANNER CAMPBELL: 1865–1940)
   English actress

◆

My favorite thing is to go where I've never been.

DIANE ARBUS (1923–71)
   American photographer

◆

Courage is the price that life exacts for granting peace.

AMELIA EARHART (1898–1937)
   *American aviator and writer who was the first woman
   to make solo flights across both the Atlantic and the Pacific*

A lady is one who never shows her underwear unintentionally.

> LILLIAN DAY (1893–)
> *American writer*

◆

All the men on my staff can type.

> BELLA ABZUG (1920–)
> *American lawyer and politician*

◆

The best time for planning a book is while you're doing the dishes.

> AGATHA CHRISTIE (1891–1975)
> *English writer and playwright*

Sometimes when I look at my children I say to myself *Lillian, you should have stayed a virgin.*

LILLIAN CARTER (1898–1983)
American nurse and Peace Corps worker, the mother of four, including Billy Carter and President Jimmy Carter

◆

Love ceases to be a pleasure when it ceases to be a secret.

APHRA BEHN (1640–89)
English playwright, poet, and writer

◆

A dress made right should allow one to walk, to dance, even to ride horseback.

COCO (GABRIELLE) CHANEL (1883–1971)
French fashion designer

A man would never get the notion of writing a book on the peculiar situation of the human male.

SIMONE DE BEAUVOIR (1908–86)
French philosopher, writer, and feminist (author of The Second Sex)

◆

I've been on a diet two weeks and all I've lost is two weeks.

TOTIE FIELDS (1931–78)
American comic

◆

Life is not always what one wants it to be, but to make the best of it as it is, is the only way of being happy.

JENNIE JEROME CHURCHILL (1854–1921)
*American-English hostess, editor, and playwright,
the mother of Winston Churchill*

Expect nothing.
Blame nobody.
Do something.

MOTTO FROM CROSS-STITCH SAMPLER

◆

Eternity is not something that begins after you are dead. It is going on all the time. We are in it now.

CHARLOTTE PERKINS GILMAN (1860–1935)
American poet, writer, and social critic

◆

I will lay down for my God, and for my kingdom, and for my people, my honor and my blood, even in the dust. I know I have but the body of a weak and feeble woman, but I have the heart and stomach of a king, and of a king of England, too.

ELIZABETH I (1533–1603)
(from a speech to an army of Englishmen
gathered to resist a Spanish invasion)
Queen of England from 1558 to 1603

◆

Never go to bed mad. Stay up and fight.

PHYLLIS DILLER (1917–)
American comic and writer

People call me a feminist whenever I express sentiments that differentiate me from a doormat or a prostitute.

REBECCA WEST (1892–1983)
Scottish-English writer

◆

I take issue with [the] premise that all men, without exception, are intruding vandals bent only on the oppression of womankind. I submit that some of them can be welcome guests.

JANE HOWARD (1935–)
American writer

◆

Love doesn't just sit there, like a stone, it has to be made, like bread; remade all the time, made new.

URSULA K. LE GUIN (1929–)
American writer and critic

Millions long for immortality who don't know what to do on a rainy Sunday afternoon.

SUSAN ERTZ (1894–1985)
American writer

◆

You cannot shake hands with a clenched fist.

INDIRA GANDHI (1917–84)
Indian politician who was the first woman elected prime minister of India

◆

There was a time when patience ceased to be a virtue. It was long ago.

CHARLOTTE PERKINS GILMAN (1860–1935)
(comment on the fact that women still could not vote)
American poet, writer, and social critic

Can you imagine a world without men:
No crime and lots of happy fat women.

NICOLE HOLLANDER (1940–)
American cartoonist

◆

I may be arrested, I may be tried and thrown in jail, but I will never be silent.

EMMA GOLDMAN (1869–1940)
Russian-American anarchist, social reformer, lecturer, and editor

◆

No man, not even a doctor, ever gives any other definition of what a nurse should be than this— "devoted and obedient." This definition would do just as well for a porter. It might even do for a horse.

FLORENCE NIGHTINGALE (1820–1910)
English nurse and writer who founded the nursing profession

Better that a girl has beauty than brains because boys see better than they think.

ANONYMOUS

◆

Once in a cabinet [meeting] we had to deal with the fact that there had been an outbreak of assaults on women at night. One minister suggested a curfew: women should stay at home after dark. I said, "But it's the men who are attacking the women. If there's to be a curfew, let the men stay home, not the women."

GOLDA MEIR (1898–1978)
Russian-American-Israeli politician who was the first female prime minister of Israel

Sometimes I'm in Washington, then in Pennsylvania, Arizona, Texas, Alabama, Colorado, Minnesota. My address is like my shoes. It travels with me. I abide where there is a fight against wrong.

MOTHER (MARY HARRIS) JONES (1830–1930)
Irish-American labor organizer and humanitarian

◆

Why should I paint dead fish, onions, and beer glasses? Girls are so much prettier.

MARIE LAURENCIN (1885–1956)
French painter

◆

I keep my campaign promises, but I never promised to wear stockings.

ELLA GRASSO (1919–81)
Politician who was the first American woman elected in her own right as governor of a state (Connecticut)

Don't compromise yourself. You're all you've got.

JANIS JOPLIN (1943–70)
American singer and songwriter

◆

I have a simple philosophy. Fill what's empty.
Empty what's full. Scratch where it itches.

ALICE ROOSEVELT LONGWORTH (1884–1980)
American wit and hostess

◆

In politics women type the letters, lick the stamps,
distribute the pamphlets, and get out the vote.
Men get elected.

CLARE BOOTHE LUCE (1903–87)
American playwright, writer, politician, and diplomat

There are two ways of spreading light: to be the candle or the mirror that receives it.

EDITH WHARTON (1862–1937)
American writer

◆

A woman's two cents is worth two cents in the music business.

LORETTA LYNN (1930–)
American singer

◆

Every society honors its live conformists and its dead troublemakers.

MIGNON McLAUGHLIN (1915–)
American writer

You'd be surprised how much it costs to look this cheap.

DOLLY PARTON (1946–)
American singer, songwriter, and actress

◆

I am not willing, now or in the future, to bring bad trouble to people who, in my past association with them, were completely innocent of any talk or any action that was disloyal or subversive. I cannot and will not cut my conscience to fit this year's fashions.

LILLIAN HELLMAN (1906–84)
(from a 1952 letter to the House Committee on Un-American Activities in which she refused to cooperate with its witch-hunt search for subversive political activity by testifying about her friends)
American playwright and writer

If you have enough courage, you don't need a reputation.

MARGARET MITCHELL (1900–49)
(Rhett Butler's advice to Scarlett O'Hara in
Mitchell's novel *Gone With The Wind*)
American writer

◆

I wonder what Adam and Eve think of it by this time.

MARIANNE MOORE (1887–1972)
(comment regarding marriage)
American poet

◆

I base my fashion taste on what doesn't itch.

GILDA RADNER (1946–89)
American comic

A woman, even a brilliant woman, must have two qualities in order to fulfill her promise: more energy than ordinary mortals, and the ability to outwit her culture.

MARGARET MEAD (1901–78)
American anthropologist, curator, and writer

◆

I ask no favor for my sex. I surrender not our claim to equality. All I ask our brethren is that they will take their heels from our necks and permit us to stand upright on that ground which God designed us to occupy.

SARAH GRIMKÉ (1792–1873)
American suffragist and abolitionist

Sex appeal is 50 percent what you've got and 50 percent what people think you've got.

SOPHIA LOREN (1934–)
Italian actress

◆

Genius is of small use to a woman who does not know how to do her hair.

EDITH WHARTON (1862–1937)
American writer

◆

If he can talk, I'll take him.

MAE WEST (1892–1980)
(comment regarding Cary Grant when she was casting the male lead for her movie *She Done Him Wrong*)
American actress and playwright

We are told that the social gap between the sexes is narrowing, but I can only report that having experienced life in both roles, there seems to me to be no aspect of existence, no moment of the day, no contact, no arrangement, no response, which is not different for men and for women.

JAN MORRIS (1926–) (born a man, James Morris)
English historian and travel writer

◆

It's easy to be independent when you've got money. But to be independent when you haven't got a thing—that's the Lord's test.

MAHALIA JACKSON (1911–72)
African-American singer

Age is something that doesn't matter, unless you are a cheese.

BILLIE BURKE (1885–1970)
American actress

◆

By the time you swear you're his
Shivering and sighing,
And he vows his passion is
Infinite, undying—
Lady, make a note of this:
One of you is lying.

DOROTHY PARKER (1893–1967)
American wit, poet, and writer

I would even go to Washington, which is saying something for me, just to glimpse Jane Q. Public being sworn in as the first female president of the United States, while her husband holds the Bible and wears a silly pillbox hat and matching coat.

ANNA QUINDLEN (1952–)
American writer

◆

One day I was tired and just wanted to get finished with the race. That's when I broke the world record for the first time. I was as shocked as everybody else.

WILMA RUDOLPH (1940–)
African-American athlete who, although she could not walk until age eight, won three gold medals and set two world records within an hour and a half at the 1960 Rome Olympics

I refuse to believe that trading recipes is silly. Tuna-fish casserole is at least as real as corporate stock.

BARBARA GRIZZUTI HARRISON (1941–)
American writer

◆

I'll try anything once.

ALICE ROOSEVELT LONGWORTH (1884–1980)
(comment on giving birth for the first time at 41)
American wit and hostess

◆

We were dispossessed by the law as a "public nuisance" [in the United States]. In Holland the [birth control] clinics were called "public utilities."

MARGARET SANGER (1883–1966)
American nurse, birth control crusader, and writer,
the founder of Planned Parenthood of America

◆

You have put me here a cub, but I will come out roaring like a lion, and I will make all hell howl.

CARRY NATION (1846–1911)
(remark made from jail after her arrest for breach of the peace)
Militant American prohibitionist, writer, and lecturer who promoted
temperance reform by smashing up saloons with a hatchet

My only concern was to get home after a hard day's work.

ROSA PARKS (1913–)
African-American domestic worker and civil rights activist whose refusal to move to the back of an Alabama bus triggered the modern American civil rights movement

◆

In a word, I am always busy, which is perhaps the chief reason I am always well.

ELIZABETH CADY STANTON (1815–1902)
American suffragist, abolitionist, lecturer, writer, and mother of seven children

◆

I can't mate in captivity.

GLORIA STEINEM (1934–)
(remark explaining why she never married)
American feminist, writer, and editor

I felt that one had better die fighting against injustice than to die like a dog or a rat in a trap. I had already determined to sell my life as dearly as possible if attacked. I felt if I could take one lyncher with me, this would even the score a bit.

IDA B. WELLS (1862–1942)
(comment concerning her attitude toward the mob
that sacked her newspaper office in retaliation for her
anti-lynching editorial campaign)
African-American abolitionist, publisher, and writer

◆

From birth to age 18 a girl needs good parents, from 18 to 35 she needs good looks, from 35 to 55 she needs a good personality, and from 55 on she needs cash.

SOPHIE TUCKER (1884–1966)
Russian-American singer

I've married a few people I shouldn't have, but haven't we all?

MAMIE VAN DOREN (1933–)
American actress

◆

I do not believe that women are better than men. We have not wrecked railroads, nor corrupted legislatures, nor done many unholy things that men have done; but then we must remember that we have not had the chance.

JANE ADDAMS (1860–1935)
American social worker who won the 1931 Nobel Peace Prize for her work among the poor of Chicago

I used to be Snow White, but I drifted.

MAE WEST (1892–1980)
American actress and playwright

◆

Whatever women do they must do twice as well as men to be thought half as good. Luckily, this is not difficult.

CHARLOTTE WHITTON (1896–1975)
(comment on being inaugurated as the first female mayor of Ottawa)
Canadian politician and writer

◆

Give us bread, but give us roses.

CRY OF NINETEENTH-CENTURY (FEMALE) NEW ENGLAND TEXTILE WORKERS, STRIKING FOR HIGHER WAGES

When, however, one reads of a witch being ducked, of a woman possessed by devils, of a wise woman selling herbs, or even a very remarkable man who had a mother, then I think we are on the track of a lost novelist, a suppressed poet. Indeed, I would venture to guess that Anon[ymous], who wrote so many poems without signing them, was often a woman.

VIRGINIA WOOLF (1882–1941)
English writer, critic, and publisher

◆

I don't remember any love affairs. One must keep love affairs quiet.

WALLIS SIMPSON WINDSOR (1896–1986)
American wife of Edward VIII, Duke of Windsor, for whom he abdicated the throne of England in 1936

Please let us not interfere with each other's work or play, nor let the world see private joys or disagreements. In this connection I may have to keep some place where I can go to be by myself now and then, for I cannot guarantee to endure at all times the confinements of even an attractive cage.

AMELIA EARHART (1898–1937)
(from a letter to her fiancé)
American aviator and writer who was the first woman to make solo flights across both the Atlantic and the Pacific

◆

The trouble with the rat race is that even if you win you're still a rat.

LILY TOMLIN (1936–)
American comic and actress

Remember, Ginger Rogers did everything Fred Astaire did, but she did it backwards and in high heels.

FAITH WHITTLESEY (1939–)
American lawyer and politician

◆

The first time you buy a house you see how pretty the paint is and buy it. The second time you look to see if the basement has termites. It's the same with men.

LUPE VELEZ (1910–44)
Mexican-American actress

You never see a man walking down the street with a woman who has a little pot belly and a bald spot.

ELAYNE BOOSLER (1952–)
American comic

◆

Hollywood's a place where they'll pay you a thousand dollars for a kiss and fifty cents for your soul.

MARILYN MONROE (1926–62)
American actress

◆

Among all the forms of absurd courage, the courage of girls is outstanding. Otherwise there would be fewer marriages.

COLETTE (1873–1954)
French writer

A man has to be Joe McCarthy to be called ruthless. All a woman has to do is put you on hold.

MARLO THOMAS (1943–)
American actress

◆

Conventionality is not morality. Self-righteousness is not religion. To attack the first is not to assail the last.

CHARLOTTE BRONTË (1816–55)
English writer and poet

◆

Success has killed more men than bullets.

TEXAS GUINAN (1884–1933)
American actress and nightclub owner

Women are repeatedly accused of taking things personally. I cannot see any other honest way of taking them.

MARYA MANNES (1904–)
American writer and critic

◆

I am independent! I can live alone and I love to work. Sometimes it made him furious that he could not find a chink in my armor, and there would be months when we just could not see each other, and then something I painted would bring us together again.

MARY CASSATT (1844–1926)
(comment regarding the painter Edgar Degas)
American-French painter

I do not wish [women]
to have power over men,
but over themselves.

MARY WOLLSTONECRAFT (1759–97)
English feminist and writer

◆

I ain't no lady. I'm a newspaperwoman.

HAZEL BRANNON SMITH (1914–81)
American newspaper publisher and writer

◆

I don't mind if my life goes in the service of the nation. If I die today every drop of my blood will invigorate the nation.

INDIRA GANDHI (1917–84)
(comment made the night before she was assassinated by her own Sikh bodyguard)
Indian politician who was the first female prime minister of India

◆

The queens in history compare favorably with the kings.

MATHILDA JOSLYN GAGE (1826–98)
American suffragist and writer

A woman's heart must be of such a size and no larger, else it must be pressed small, like Chinese feet.

GEORGE ELIOT (MARIAN EVANS: 1819–80)
English writer

◆

The hardest years in life are those between ten and seventy.

HELEN HAYES (1900–93)
American actress and writer

◆

Sooner or later I'm going to die, but I'm not going to retire.

MARGARET MEAD (1901–78)
American anthropologist, curator, and writer

"We, the people of the United States." Which "We, the people"? The women were not included.

LUCY STONE (1818–93)
American feminist, abolitionist, editor, and lecturer

◆

The modern rule is that every woman must be her own chaperone.

AMY VANDERBILT (1908–74)
American etiquette writer

◆

Being an old maid is like death by drowning, a really delightful sensation after you cease to struggle.

EDNA FERBER (1887–1968)
American writer

It is extremely silly to submit to ill fortune.

> MARY WORTLEY MONTAGU (1689–1762)
> *English writer*

◆

Do you think it pleases a man when he looks into a woman's eyes and sees a reflection of the English Museum Reading Room?

> MURIEL SPARK (1918–)
> *English-Scottish writer and poet*

◆

A sensible woman should never fall in love without her heart's consent, nor marry without that of her reason.

> NINON DE L'ENCLOS (1620–1705)
> *French courtesan*

Time and trouble will tame an advanced young woman, but an advanced old woman is uncontrollable by any force.

DOROTHY L. SAYERS (1893–1957)
English writer

❖

Women should try to increase their size rather than decrease it, because I believe the bigger we are, the more space we'll take up, and the more we'll have to be reckoned with. I think every woman should be fat like me.

ROSEANNE ARNOLD (1952–)
American comic, actress, and television producer

Woman is shut up in a kitchen or in a boudoir and astonishment is expressed that her horizon is limited. Her wings are clipped, and it is found deplorable that she cannot fly.

SIMONE DE BEAUVOIR (1908–86)
French philosopher, writer, and feminist

◆

I am a frayed and nibbled survivor in a fallen world and I am getting along. I am aging and eaten and have done my share of eating, too.

ANNIE DILLARD (1945–)
American writer and poet

◆

It is better to be a bad original than a good copy.

MARIE DU DEFFAND (1697–1780)
French hostess and wit

Seeing unhappiness in the marriages of friends, I was content to have chosen music and laughter as a substitute for a husband.

> ELSA MAXWELL (1883–1963)
> *American hostess, songwriter, and writer*

◆

Women are the one group left in the world which is supposed to love people who consider them inferior.

> GLORIA STEINEM (1934–)
> *American feminist, writer, and editor*

◆

In my opinion, to a woman who knows her own mind, men can be only a minor consideration.

> MARIE BASHKIRTSEFF (1860–84)
> *Russian-French artist and diarist*

Marriage is a mutual blackmail. If it has to be un-done, it just leads to a great legal event. Why shouldn't one realize that it is a temporary state? Life is temporary.

EDNA O'BRIEN (1932–)
Irish-English writer

◆

Men who are in love are not interested in whether the girl knows an A from a B at the beginning of the relationship. Afterwards they try to improve her.

SHEILAH GRAHAM (1908–88)
English-American writer

A good actress lasts. Sex attraction does not.

BRIGITTE BARDOT (1934–)
French actress

◆

What's left of her, dahling.

TALLULAH BANKHEAD (1903–68)
(in answer to the question "Are you really Tallulah Bankhead?")
American actress

◆

And I shall earnestly and persistently continue to urge all women to the practical recognition of the old Revolutionary [War] maxim, "Resistance to tyranny is obedience to God."

SUSAN B. ANTHONY (1820–1906)
American suffragist and writer

Row, you sons of bitches. Row or I'll let daylight into you!

THE UNSINKABLE MOLLY (MARGARET) BROWN (1873–1932)
(comment to her weeping (female) fellow passengers on a
Titanic lifeboat)
American social climber and philanthropist

◆

Sixty-eight is no age to give up your job.

QUEEN MARY (1867–1953)
(comment on hearing of the abdication of
Queen Wilhelmina of Holland)
*English wife of George V of England and the
grandmother of Elizabeth II*

◆

My own, or other people's?

PEGGY GUGGENHEIM (1898–1979)
(in answer to the question "How many husbands have you had?")
American heiress and art patron

I am looking for him.

MARY KINGSLEY (1862–1900)
(in answer to the frequent question from the natives she encountered during her explorations in Africa, "Where is your husband?")
(Unmarried) English explorer and writer

◆

While others argued the equality of woman and man, I proved it by successfully engaging in business. I therefore claim the right to speak for the unenfranchised women of the country, and, believing as I do that the prejudices which still exist in the popular mind against women in public life will soon disappear, I now announce myself as candidate for the presidency.

VICTORIA WOODHULL (1838–1927)
American feminist, writer, and editor who was the first female candidate for the presidency of the United States

If women want any rights they had better take them and say nothing about it.

HARRIET BEECHER STOWE (1811–96)
American abolitionist and writer

◆

You don't do that to me, my dear, I'm only in politics.

MARGARET THATCHER (1925–)
(comment to a Spanish tourist who mistakenly curtsied to her on the streets of London)
English politician who was the first female British prime minister

◆

It would be much kinder if they sent me champagne while I am alive; they can send me flowers when I am dead.

ISADORA DUNCAN (1878–1927)
American dancer, educator, and writer

◆

No matter how old a mother is she watches her middle-aged children for signs of improvement.

FLORIDA SCOTT-MAXWELL (1884–1979)
American-Scottish suffragist, psychologist, and writer

Time wasted is poison.

MAY SARTON (1912–)
Belgian-American poet and writer

◆

Trust me, my beloved friend, the mind has no sex but what habit and education give it and I who was thrown in infancy upon the world like a wreck upon the waters have learned as well to struggle with the elements as any male child of Adam.

FRANCES WRIGHT (1795–1852)
Scottish-American social reformer and writer

◆

Slow down? Rest? With all eternity before me?

SARAH BERNHARDT (1844–1923)
French actress and writer

Self-development is a higher duty than self-sacrifice.

ELIZABETH CADY STANTON (1815-1902)
American suffragist, abolitionist, lecturer, and writer

◆

I was always praying for poor old master. 'Pears like I didn't do nothing but pray for old master. "Oh, Lord, change that man's heart and make him a Christian." And all the time he was bringing men [buyers] to look at me. Then I heard that I was to be sent with my brothers in the chain-gang to the far South. Then I changed my prayer, and I said, "Lord, if you ain't never going to change that man's heart, KILL him."

HARRIET TUBMAN (1815–1913)
(comment about her life at age 14)
African-American former slave and abolitionist active in the "underground railway" for escaping slaves and as a Union spy

Pray, good people, be civil. I am the Protestant whore.

NELL GWYNN (1650–87)
(comment on being surrounded in her coach during the time of the Popish Plot by a mob shouting "It is the Catholic whore!" who thought she was the king's Catholic mistress, Louise de Keroualle)
English actress who was the mistress of Charles II

◆

Women have served all these centuries as looking glasses possessing the magic and delicious power of reflecting the figure of man at twice its natural size.

VIRGINIA WOOLF (1882–1941)
English writer, critic, and publisher

Love is a game that two can play and both win.

EVA GABOR (1921–)
Hungarian-American actress

◆

I believe it would be a great loss to the community as well as to women if talented women did not have children. They should have at least as many, if not more, children than less talented women.

ROSALYN YALOW (1921–)
American medical physicist who won the 1977 Nobel Prize for Medicine

◆

If you obey all the rules you miss all the fun.

KATHARINE HEPBURN (1909–)
American actress

I wasn't lucky. I deserved it.

MARGARET THATCHER (1925–)
(comment, at the age of nine, on winning a school prize)
English politician who was the first female British prime minister

◆

In society it is etiquette for ladies to have the best chairs and get handed things. In the home the reverse is the case. That is why ladies are more sociable than gentlemen.

VIRGINIA GRAHAM (1912–)
American writer and broadcaster

◆

Opportunities are usually disguised as hard work, so most people don't recognize them.

ANN LANDERS (1918–)
American newspaper advice columnist

I love all my children, but some of them I don't like.

LILLIAN CARTER (1898–1983)
American nurse and Peace Corps worker and the mother of four, including Billy Carter and President Jimmy Carter

◆

I do not want to die until I have faithfully made the most of my talent and cultivated the seed that was placed in me until the last small twig has grown.

KÄTHE KOLLWITZ (1867–1945)
German painter, sculptor, and graphic artist

◆

Of course you are, my dear, of course you are.

BETTE DAVIS (1908–89)
(in reply to a fan's comment "Miss Davis, I'm a great fan of yours.")
American actress

No woman can call herself free who does not own and control her body. No woman can call herself free until she can choose consciously whether she will or will not be a mother.

MARGARET SANGER (1883–1966)
American nurse, birth control crusader, and writer,
the founder of Planned Parenthood of America

◆

How idiotic civilization is! Why be given a body if you have to keep it shut up in a case like a rare, rare fiddle?

KATHERINE MANSFIELD (1888–1923)
English writer and critic

The only people who never fail are those who never try.

ILKA CHASE (1905–78)
American actress and writer

◆

Fame is a fickle food upon a shifting plate.

EMILY DICKINSON (1830–86)
American poet

◆

Anything that's natural can't be sinful—it may be inconvenient, but it's not sinful.

MADELEINE L'ENGLE (1918–)
American writer

I'll match my flops with anybody's but I wouldn't have missed 'em. Flops are a part of life's menu and I've never been a girl to miss out on any of the courses.

ROSALIND RUSSELL (1911–76)
American actress

◆

The graveyards are full of women whose houses were so spotless you could eat off the floor. Remember, the second wife always has a maid.

HELOISE CRUSE (1920–)
American household hints columnist

◆

It is better to break one's heart than to do nothing with it.

MARGARET KENNEDY (1896–1967)
English writer, playwright, and critic

Women were surely intended to be beautiful, and it is a low trick on the part of Creation to make some of them ravishing and to give Phi Beta [Kappa] keys to the rest of us as a sop.

MARJORIE KINNAN RAWLINGS (1896–1953)
American writer

◆

Happiness is not a station you arrive at, but a manner of traveling.

MARGARET LEE RUNBECK (1905–56)
American writer

That man over there says women need to be helped into carriages and lifted over ditches, and to have the best place everywhere. Nobody ever helps me into carriages or over puddles, or gives me the best place—and ain't I a woman? Look at this arm! I have ploughed and planted and gathered into barns, and no man could head me—and ain't I a woman? I could work as much and eat as much as a man—when I could get it—and bear the lash as well. And ain't I a woman? I have borne thirteen children, and seen most of 'em sold off to slavery, and when I cried out with my mother's grief, none but Jesus heard me—*and ain't I a woman?*

SOJOURNER TRUTH (1797–1883)
(from a speech at a women's rights convention)
African-American abolitionist and feminist, a former slave

What a holler would ensue, if people had to pay the minister as much to marry them as they have to pay a lawyer to get them a divorce.

CLAIRE TREVOR (1909–)
American actress

◆

There is no slave, after all, like a wife. Women sell themselves and are sold in marriage, from queens downward. Poor women, poor slaves.

MARY CHESNUT (1823–86)
American Civil War diarist

◆

Love is moral even without legal marriage, but marriage is immoral without love.

ELLEN KEY (1845–1926)
Swedish writer and feminist

There is so little difference between husbands you might as well keep the first.

ADELA ROGERS ST. JOHNS (1894–1988)
American writer

Progress in civilization has been accompanied by progress in cookery.

FANNIE FARMER (1857–1915)
American chef and writer

◆

So many persons think divorce a panacea for every ill, who find out, when they try it, that the remedy is worse than the disease.

DOROTHY DIX (1861–1951)
American writer

◆

Men their rights and nothing more; women their rights and nothing less.

SUSAN B. ANTHONY (1820–1906)
(motto of her women's suffrage newspaper, *The Revolution*)
American suffragist and editor

The single most impressive fact about the attempt by American women to obtain the right to vote is how long it took.

ALICE ROSSI (1922–)
American sociologist, educator, and editor

◆

I love my past. I love my present. I'm not ashamed of what I've had, and I'm not sad because I have it no longer.

COLETTE (1873–1954)
French writer

◆

There are those who say I'm impatient, impetuous, uppity, rude, profane, brash, and overbearing, but whatever I am, I am a very serious woman.

BELLA ABZUG (1920–)
American lawyer and politician

As I grow older and older and totter towards the tomb, I find that I care less and less who goes to bed with whom.

DOROTHY L. SAYERS (1893–1957)
English writer

◆

It is delightful to be a woman, but every man thanks the lord devoutly that he is not one.

OLIVE SCHREINER (1855–1920)
South African social critic, writer, and feminist

◆

Spinsterhood is powerful; once a woman is called "that crazy old maid" she can get away with anything.

FLORENCE KING (1936–)
American writer

I am not saying that in order to write well, or think well, it is necessary to become unavailable to others, or to become a devouring ego. This has been the myth of the masculine artist and thinker, and I do not accept it.

ADRIENNE RICH (1929–)
American poet

◆

Slavery made us tough.

FRANCES HARPER (1825–1911)
(comment on the ability of former slaves to survive during Reconstruction)
African-American poet, lecturer, and reformer

I don't think of all the misery, but of the beauty that still remains. My advice is: Go outside to the fields, enjoy nature and the sunshine, try to recapture happiness in yourself and in God.

ANNE FRANK (1929–45)
(Jewish) German diarist who died, at age 16, in a concentration camp after hiding from the Nazis in an attic with her family

◆

Light tomorrow with today!

ELIZABETH BARRETT BROWNING (1806–61)
English poet

◆

Whenever you want to marry someone, go have lunch with his ex-wife.

SHELLY WINTERS (1922–)
American actress

Being a housewife and a mother is the biggest job in the world, but if it doesn't interest you, don't do it. I would have made a terrible mother.

KATHARINE HEPBURN (1909–)
American actress

◆

No time to marry, no time to settle down; I'm a young woman, and I ain't done runnin' aroun'.

BESSIE SMITH (1898–1937)
African-American singer and songwriter

◆

The way you overcome shyness is to become so wrapped up in something that you forget to be afraid.

LADY BIRD (CLAUDIA) JOHNSON (1912–)
American First Lady and wildflower conservationist, the widow of President Lyndon Johnson

For fast-acting relief, try slowing down.

LILY TOMLIN (1936–)
American comic and actress

◆

What is important is to keep learning, to enjoy challenge, and to tolerate ambiguity. In the end there are no certain answers.

MATINA HORNER (1929–)
American psychiatrist, educator, and writer

◆

This is not a democracy. It's a queendom.

ROSEANNE ARNOLD (1952–)
(remark to the staff of her television show)
American comic, actress, and television producer

When I'm ready to stop acting, you'll read about it in the obituaries.

JESSICA TANDY (1909–)
American actress

◆

The executioner is, I believe, an expert and my neck is very slender. Oh, God, have pity on my soul.

ANNE BOLEYN (1507–36)
(her last words before she was beheaded, with an ax)
English aristocrat, the second wife and queen to Henry VIII of England, who had her beheaded in order to marry the third of his eight wives; the mother of Elizabeth I of England

If pregnancy were a book, they would cut the last two chapters.

NORA EPHRON (1941–)
American writer and movie director

◆

Women's virtue is man's greatest invention.

CORNELIA OTIS SKINNER (1901–79)
American writer and actress

◆

Let other pens dwell on guilt and misery.

JANE AUSTEN (1775–1817)
English writer

Standing, as I do, in the view of God and eternity,
I realize that patriotism is not enough. I must have
no hatred or bitterness towards anyone.

EDITH CAVELL (1865–1915)
(her last words, spoken to the chaplain who attended her before
her execution by a German firing squad)
English nurse who was executed as an Allied spy during World War I

◆

My candle burns at both its ends;
It will not last the night;
But oh, my foes, and oh, my friends—
It gives a lovely light.

EDNA ST. VINCENT MILLAY (1892–1952)
American poet, playwright, and writer

In a dream you are never eighty.

ANNE SEXTON (1928–74)
American poet

◆

It is not easy to find happiness in ourselves, and it is not possible to find it elsewhere.

AGNES REPPLIER (1858–1950)
American writer and social critic

◆

Courage! I have shown it for years; think you I shall lose it at the moment when my sufferings are to end?

MARIE ANTOINETTE (1755–93)
(remark as she rode to the guillotine)
French aristocrat who was wife and queen to Louis XVI of France; beheaded during the French Revolution

Move Queen Anne? Most certainly not! Why it might some day be suggested that my statue should be moved, which I should much dislike.

QUEEN VICTORIA (1819–1901)
(comment when it was suggested that a statue of Queen Anne should be moved)
Queen of England from 1837 to 1901 and the person who gave her name to the "Victorian" era

◆

Art is the only thing that can go on mattering once it has stopped hurting.

ELIZABETH BOWEN (1899–1973)
Irish-English writer

One must choose in life between boredom and suffering.

GERMAINE DE STAËL (1766–1817)
French writer

◆

I never married because I have three pets at home that answer the same purpose as a husband. I have a dog that growls every morning, a parrot that swears all afternoon, and a cat that comes home late at night.

MARIE CORELLI (1855–1924)
English writer

◆

The thing about having a baby is that thereafter you have it.

JEAN KERR (1923–)
American playwright and writer

If the world were a logical place, men would ride sidesaddle.

RITA MAE BROWN (1944–)
American writer and poet

◆

It doesn't matter what you do in the bedroom as long as you don't do it in the streets and frighten the horses.

MRS. PATRICK CAMPBELL
(BEATRICE STELLA TANNER CAMPBELL: 1865–1940)
English actress

◆

Chivalry is a poor substitute for justice, if one cannot have both. Chivalry is something like the icing on cake, sweet, but not nourishing.

NELLIE MCCLUNG (1873–1951)
Canadian feminist and writer

◆

Macho does not prove mucho.

ZSA ZSA GABOR (1919–)
Hungarian-American actress

When I'm good, I'm very good, but when I'm bad, I'm better.

MAE WEST (1892–1980)
American actress and playwright

◆

Make it a rule of life never to regret and never to look back. Regret is an appalling waste of energy; you can't build on it, it's good only for wallowing in.

KATHERINE MANSFIELD (1888–1923)
English writer

◆

Whatever else can be said about sex, it cannot be called a dignified performance.

HELEN LAWRENSON (1907–82)
American writer

Women keep a special corner of their hearts for sins they have never committed.

CORNELIA OTIS SKINNER (1901–79)
American actress and writer

◆

I wasn't allowed to speak while my husband was alive, and since he's gone no one has been able to shut me up.

HEDDA HOPPER (1890–1966)
American gossip columnist

◆

What does my hair-do have to do with my husband's ability to be president?

JACQUELINE KENNEDY ONASSIS (1929–)
American editor and socialite who was the wife of President John F. Kennedy

I can't be a rose in any man's lapel.

MARGARET TRUDEAU (1948–)
Former wife of Canadian Prime Minister Pierre Trudeau

◆

Sometimes I wonder if men and women really suit each other. Perhaps they should live next door and just visit now and then.

KATHARINE HEPBURN (1909–)
American actress

◆

Throughout history, females have picked providers for mates. Males pick anything.

MARGARET MEAD (1901–78)
American anthropologist and writer

If someone is dumb enough to offer me a million dollars to make a picture I am certainly not dumb enough to turn it down.

ELIZABETH TAYLOR (1932–)
English-American actress

◆

In Hollywood all marriages are happy. It's trying to live together afterward that causes problems.

SHELLEY WINTERS (1922–)
American actress

◆

Everything you see I owe to spaghetti.

SOPHIA LOREN (1934–)
Italian actress

We're half the people; we should be half the Congress.

JEANNETTE RANKIN (1880–1973)
American pacifist, feminist, and politician; the first woman elected to the U.S. Congress

◆

I have no dress except the one I wear every day. If you are going to be kind enough to give me one, please let it be practical and dark so that I can put it on afterwards to go to the laboratory.

MARIE CURIE (1867–1934)
(from a letter to a friend referring to an offer of a dress for her wedding to Pierre Curie)
Polish-French scientist who won the 1903 Nobel Prize for Physics and the 1911 Nobel Prize for Chemistry

I can hold a note as long as the Chase National Bank.

ETHEL MERMAN (1909–84)
American singer and actress

◆

There are an awful lot of skinny people in the cemetary.

BEVERLY SILLS (1929–)
American singer

◆

In our family we don't divorce our men—we bury them.

RUTH GORDON (1896–1985)
American actress and playwright

Before marriage a man will lie awake all night thinking about something you said; after marriage he will fall asleep before you have finished saying it.

HELEN ROWLAND (1876–1950)
American writer and humorist

◆

Disgraceful, I know, but I can't help choosing my underwear with a view to its being seen.

BARBARA PYM (1913–80)
English writer

◆

I am what you call a hooligan!

EMMELINE PANKHURST (1858–1928)
English suffragist who was often arrested for demonstrating for votes for women

All one's life as a young woman one is on show, a focus of attention, people notice you. You set yourself up to be noticed and admired. And then, not expecting it, you become middle-aged and anonymous. No one notices you. You achieve a wonderful freedom. It is a positive thing. You can move about, unnoticed and invisible.

DORIS LESSING (1919–)
English writer and playwright

◆

You cannot make yourself feel something you do not feel, but you can make yourself do right in spite of your feelings.

PEARL S. BUCK (1892–1973)
(advice to her daughter)
American writer who won the 1938 Nobel Prize for Literature

Flirtation is merely an expression of considered desire coupled with an admission of its impracticability.

MARYA MANNES (1904–)
American writer

◆

It is ridiculous to think you can spend your entire life with one person. Three is about the right number. Yes, I imagine three husbands would do it.

CLARE BOOTHE LUCE (1903–87)
American playwright, writer, politician, and diplomat

◆

Life is something to do when you can't get to sleep.

FRAN LEBOWITZ (1951–)
American writer and humorist

Whose love is given over-well
Shall look on Helen's face in hell
Whilst those whose love is thin and wise
May view John Knox in paradise.

> DOROTHY PARKER (1893–1967)
> *American wit, poet, and writer*

◆

The great and almost only comfort about being a woman is that one can always pretend to be more stupid than one is, and no one is surprised.

> FREYA STARK (1893–)
> *French-English traveller and writer*

◆

No matter what your fight, don't be ladylike.

> MOTHER (MARY HARRIS) JONES (1830–1930)
> *Irish-American labor organizer and humanitarian*

I read Shakespeare
and the Bible, and I can
shoot dice. That's what
I call a liberal education.

TALLULAH BANKHEAD (1903–68)
American actress

◆

I certainly am glad you like the stories because now I feel it's not bad that I like them so much. The truth is I like them better than anybody and I read them over and over and laugh and laugh, then get embarrassed when I remember I was the one wrote them.

FLANNERY O'CONNOR (1925–64)
(from a letter to a correspondent who liked her short stories)
American writer

◆

I can trust my husband not to fall asleep on a public platform and he usually claps in the right places.

MARGARET THATCHER (1925–)
English politician who was the first female British prime minister

I refuse to admit that I am more than fifty-two, even if that does make my sons illegitimate.

> NANCY ASTOR (1879–1964)
> *American-English politician, the first woman elected to the British House of Commons*

◆

I myself prefer my New Zealand eggs for breakfast.

> ELIZABETH II (1926–)
> (comment after she was pelted with eggs during a trip to New Zealand)
> *Queen of England since 1952*

◆

I've been on a constant diet for the last two decades. I've lost a total of 789 pounds. By all accounts, I should be hanging from a charm bracelet.

> ERMA BOMBECK (1927–)
> *American writer and humorist*

[That man in black says] woman can't have as much rights as man because Christ wasn't a woman. Where did your Christ come from? From God and a woman. Man had nothing to do with it.

SOJOURNER TRUTH (1797–1883)
(comment referring to a clergyman in the audience at a women's rights convention where she was speaking)
African-American abolitionist and feminist, a former slave

◆

It's not the tragedies that kill us, it's the messes.

DOROTHY PARKER (1893–1967)
American wit, poet, and writer

◆

Good communication is as stimulating as black coffee and just as hard to sleep after.

ANNE MORROW LINDBERGH (1906–93)
American aviator, writer, and poet

I have been told there's no precedent for admitting a woman to practice in the Supreme Court of the United States. The glory of each generation is to make its own precedents. As there was none for Eve in the Garden of Eden, so there need be none for her daughters on entering the colleges, the church, or the courts.

BELVA LOCKWOOD (1830–1917)
American feminist and lawyer who was the first woman to practice before the U.S. Supreme Court

◆

What I really do is to take real plums and put them into an imaginary cake.

MARY MCCARTHY (1912–89)
(comment on her writing)
American writer, critic, and editor

Was it for this I uttered prayers,
And sobbed and cursed and kicked the stairs,
That now, domestic as a plate,
I should retire at half-past eight?

EDNA ST. VINCENT MILLAY (1892–1950)
American poet and playwright

◆

If you have formed the habit of checking on every new diet that comes along, you will find that, mercifully, they all blur together, leaving you with only one definite piece of information: french-fried potatoes are out.

JEAN KERR (1923–)
American playwright and writer

When one door of happiness closes, another opens; but often we look so long at the closed door that we do not see the one which has been opened for us.

HELEN KELLER (1880–1968)
American writer and lecturer who was blind and deaf from birth

◆

Though I know he loves me,
Tonight my heart is sad;
His kiss was not so wonderful
As all the dreams I had.

SARA TEASDALE (1884–1933)
American poet

◆

If I didn't start painting, I would have raised chickens.

GRANDMA (ANNA) MOSES (1860–1961)
American painter

A woman has got to love a bad man once or twice in her life to be thankful for a good one.

MARJORIE KINNAN RAWLINGS (1896–1953)
American writer

◆

It is often said that chivalry will disappear from the world if women start to live by their own efforts. To this I can only say that [a] chivalry in which one first binds fast the legs of the object of one's homage in order to serve her seems to me of scant value, and that it would be more chivalrous to cut the bonds. I think there ought to be far more chivalry among people of the same sex, among friends and colleagues, than there is now.

ISAK DINESEN (KAREN BLIXEN: 1885–1962)
Danish writer

If a trash can had a [light]bulb, I played it.

JOAN RIVERS (1939–)
(comment on the early days of her career)
American comic and talk-show host

◆

Certainly it [has] never occurred to designers of male garments to order men to wear polka-dot suits one year and plaid suits the next; to wear short pants to the office and kilts to dinner and sleeveless suits on the street.

EDNA FERBER (1887–1968)
American writer

Not only are you responsible for your life, but doing the best at this moment puts you in the best place for the next moment.

OPRAH WINFREY (1954–)
American talk-show host and actress

◆

And when her biographer says of an Italian woman poet, "during some years her Muse was intermitted," we do not wonder at the fact when he casually mentions her ten children.

ANNA GARLIN SPENCER (1851–1931)
American social reformer

◆

Marriage removes the illusion, deeply imbedded previously, that somewhere there is a soul-mate.

PAULA MODERSOHN-BECKER (1876–1907)
German painter

As a woman, I can't go to war, and I refuse to send anyone else.

JEANNETTE RANKIN (1880–1973)
American pacifist, feminist, and politician; the first woman elected to the U.S. Congress, and the only person to vote against the United States' entry into both World War I and World War II

◆

In many important ways women are often smarter than men. They have had to be smarter in order to survive. [Women] for centuries [were] held in subjection. Hounded and bedeviled and persecuted, granted few rights and fewer privileges, they learned perforce to see through the back of their heads. This special gift came to be known as intuition.

EDNA FERBER (1887–1968)
American writer

No one can make you feel inferior without your consent.

ELEANOR ROOSEVELT (1884–1962)
American First Lady, humanitarian, and writer, the wife of President Franklin Roosevelt

◆

A husband is what is left of the lover after the nerve has been extracted.

HELEN ROWLAND (1876–1950)
American humorist and writer

◆

In case of necessity, I shall have myself strapped to the scenery.

SARAH BERNHARDT (1844–1923)
(remark at age 76 when, because she was sick and had lost one leg, someone inquired about her ability to keep performing)
French actress and writer

Show me a woman who doesn't feel guilty and I'll show you a man.

ERICA JONG (1943–)
American writer and poet

◆

I will make a battering-ram of my head and make a way through this rough-and-tumble world.

LOUISA MAY ALCOTT (1832–88)
(comment at age 20)
American writer and editor

◆

I doubt if there'll be any true women's liberation until women are paid for bringing up children, which I think should carry a salary with it.

LILLIAN HELLMAN (1906–84)
American writer and playwright

◆

Nothing contributes so much to tranquilizing the mind as a steady purpose—a point on which the soul may fix its intellectual eye.

MARY SHELLEY (1797–1851)
English writer

It is easier to live through someone else than to become complete yourself.

BETTY FRIEDAN (1921–)
American feminist and writer who founded the National Organization for Women

◆

That's the trouble, a sex symbol becomes a thing. I just hate being a thing.

MARILYN MONROE (1926–62)
American actress

◆

I am here and you will know that I am the best and will hear me. The color of my skin or the kink of my hair or the spread of my mouth has nothing to do with what you are listening to.

LEONTYNE PRICE (1927–)
African-American singer

By and large, mothers and housewives are the only workers who do not have regular time off. They are the great vacationless class.

ANNE MORROW LINDBERGH (1906–93)
American aviator, writer, and poet

◆

With any child entering adolescence, one is desperate for the smallest indication that the child's problems will never be important enough for a television movie.

DELIA EPHRON (1944–)
American writer and humorist

◆

Another belief of mine: that everyone else my age is an adult, whereas I am merely in disguise.

MARGARET ATWOOD (1939–)
Canadian writer and poet

After thirty, a body has a mind of its own.

BETTE MIDLER (1945–)
American singer and actress

◆

Paradoxical as it may seem, to believe in youth is to look backward; to look forward we must believe in age.

DOROTHY L. SAYERS (1893–1957)
English writer

◆

It seems to me that since I've had children, I've grown richer and deeper. They may have slowed down my writing for a while, but when I did write, I had more of a self to speak from.

ANNE TYLER (1941–)
American writer

You see an awful lot of smart guys with dumb women, but you hardly ever see a smart woman with a dumb guy.

ERICA JONG (1943–)
American writer and poet

◆

One day I found myself saying to myself *I can't live where I want to, I can't go where I want to, I can't do what I want to. I can't even say what I want to.* I decided I was a very stupid fool not to at least paint as I wanted to and say what I wanted to when I painted, and that seemed to be the only thing I could do that didn't concern anybody but myself.

GEORGIA O'KEEFFE (1887–1986)
American painter

No laborer in the world is expected to work for room, board, and love except the housewife.

LETTY COTTIN POGREBIN (1939–)
American writer and editor

◆

Art is the only thing you cannot punch a button for. You must do it the old-fashioned way. Stay up and really burn the midnight oil. There are no compromises.

LEONTYNE PRICE (1927–)
African-American singer

◆

Leaving behind books is even more beautiful— there are far too many children.

MARGUERITE YOURCENAR (1903–87)
French-American writer

The grim possibility is that she who "hides her brains" will, more than likely, end up with a mate who is only equal to a woman with "hidden brains" or none at all.

LORRAINE HANSBERRY (1930–65)
African-American playwright

◆

A happy woman is one who has no cares at all; a cheerful woman is one who has cares but doesn't let them get her down.

BEVERLY SILLS (1929–)
American singer

◆

I buried a lot of my ironing in the back yard.

PHYLLIS DILLER (1917–)
American comic and writer

Adorable children are considered to be the general property of the human race. Rude children belong to their mothers.

MISS MANNERS (JUDITH MARTIN: 1938–)
American etiquette writer

◆

To be a hero, one must give an order to oneself.

SIMONE WEIL (1909–43)
French revolutionary, writer, and philosopher

◆

You are a member of the English royal family. We are *never* tired, and we all *love* hospitals.

QUEEN MARY (1867–1953)
(comment to Queen Elizabeth II)
English wife of George V of England and grandmother of Elizabeth II of England

I can never remember being afraid of an audience.
If the audience could do better, they'd be up here
on stage and I'd be out there watching them.

ETHEL MERMAN (1909–84)
American singer and actress

◆

Tremendous amounts of talent are being lost to
our society just because that talent wears a skirt.

SHIRLEY CHISHOLM (1924–)
African-American politician and writer

◆

I have everything now I had twenty years ago—
except now it's all lower.

GYPSY ROSE LEE (1914–70)
American striptease artist

Having been alive, it won't be hard in the end to lie down and rest.

PEARL BAILEY (1918–)
African-American singer

◆

I have always detested the belief that sex is the chief bond between man and woman. Friendship is far more human.

AGNES SMEDLEY (1894–1950)
American writer and lecturer

◆

When the Syrian ambassador acted up, what I really felt like saying to him was, "Go to your room!"

JEANNE J. KIRKPATRICK (1926–)
American educator and politician who was
United States ambassador to the United Nations

Personally I know nothing about sex because I've always been married.

ZSA ZSA GABOR (1919–)
Hungarian-American actress

◆

I'm tired of everlastingly being unnatural and never doing anything I want to do. I'm tired of acting like I don't eat more than a bird, and walking when I want to run and saying I feel faint after a waltz, when I could dance for two days and never get tired. I'm tired of saying "How wonderful you are!" to fool men who haven't got one-half the sense I've got and I'm tired of pretending I don't know anything, so men can tell me things and feel important while they're doing it.

MARGARET MITCHELL (1900–49)
(spoken by Scarlett O'Hara in Mitchell's novel *Gone With The Wind*)
American writer

Life is easier to take
than you'd think;
all that is necessary is to
accept the impossible,
do without the indispensable,
and bear the intolerable.

KATHLEEN NORRIS (1880–1966)
American writer

One advantage of marriage, it seems to me, is that when you fall out of love with him, or he falls out of love with you, it keeps you together until you maybe fall in again.

JUDITH VIORST (1935–)
American poet and writer

◆

Always be on time. Do as little talking as humanly possible. Remember to lean back in the parade car so everybody can see the president. Be sure not to get too fat, because you'll have to sit three in the back seat.

ELEANOR ROOSEVELT (1884–1962)
(remark on campaign behavior for First Ladies)
American First Lady, humanitarian, and writer,
the wife of President Franklin Roosevelt

The bitterest tears shed over graves are for words left unsaid and deeds left undone.

HARRIET BEECHER STOWE (1811–96)
American abolitionist and writer

◆

Talent is helpful in writing, but guts are absolutely necessary.

JESSAMYN WEST (1907–)
American writer

◆

It is the simple things of life that make living worthwhile, the sweet fundamental things such as love and duty, work and rest, and living close to nature.

LAURA INGALLS WILDER (1867–1957)
American writer

I was elected by the women of Ireland, who instead of rocking the cradle, rocked the system.

MARY ROBINSON (1944–)
Irish politician who is the first female president of Ireland

◆

A human being must have occupation if he or she is not to become a nuisance to the world.

DOROTHY L. SAYERS (1893–1957)
English writer

◆

We're half the people; we should be half the Congress.

JEANNETTE RANKIN (1880–1973)
American pacifist, feminist, and politician; the first woman elected to the U.S. Congress

I long to hear that you have declared an independency—and by the way in the new Code of Laws which I suppose it will be necessary for you to make I desire you would Remember the Ladies, and be more generous and favorable to them than your ancestors. Do not put such unlimited power into the hands of the Husbands. Remember all Men would be tyrants if they could. If particular care and attention is not paid to the Ladies we are determined to foment a Rebellion, and will not hold ourselves bound by any Laws in which we have no voice, or Representation. That your Sex are Naturally Tyrannical is a Truth so thoroughly established as to admit of no dispute, but such of you as wish to be happy willingly give up the harsh title of Master for the more tender and endearing one of Friend.

ABIGAIL ADAMS (1744–1818)
(from a letter to her husband)
American First Lady and writer, the wife of President John Adams

I never wanted to get married. The last thing I wanted was infinite security, and to be the place an arrow shoots off from. I wanted change and excitement and to shoot off in all directions myself, like the colored arrows from a Fourth of July rocket.

SYLVIA PLATH (1932–63)
American poet and writer

◆

The children will not leave unless I do. I shall not leave unless their father does, and the King will not leave the country in any circumstances whatever.

QUEEN ELIZABETH (1900–)
(comment regarding her refusal to leave Buckingham Palace during the German bombing of London during World War II)
Wife of George VI of England and mother of Elizabeth II of England

Senator, I am one of them. You do not seem to understand who I am. I am a black woman, the daughter of a dining-car worker. If my life has any meaning at all, it is that those who start out as outcasts can wind up as part of the system.

PATRICIA ROBERTS HARRIS (1924–85)
(reply during her confirmation hearings to the question whether she would be able to defend the interests of the poor as Secretary of Housing and Urban Development)
American lawyer and politician

◆

I never thought of stopping, and I just hated sleeping. I can't imagine having a better life.

BARBARA MCCLINTOCK (1902–)
(comment on her lifelong research into the genetic characteristics of corn plants)
American scientist who won the 1983 Nobel Prize for Medicine

The best contraceptive is the word *no*— repeated frequently.

MARGARET CHASE SMITH (1897–)
American politician

◆

I am a little pencil in the hand of a writing God who is sending a love letter to the world.

MOTHER TERESA (1910–)
Yugoslavian Catholic nun and missionary who won the 1979 Nobel Peace Prize for her work in the slums of Calcutta

◆

I've never seen a Brink's truck follow a hearse to the cemetery.

BARBARA HUTTON (1912–)
(comment on being told that she was being exploited)
American heiress

I forgave the D.A.R. many years ago. You lose a lot of time hating people.

MARIAN ANDERSON (1902–)
(comment made 25 years after the Daughters of the American Revolution refused her concert space in Washington, D.C.'s Constitution Hall because of her color)
African-American singer

◆

For the happiest life, days should be rigorously planned, nights left open to chance.

MIGNON MCLAUGHLIN (1915–)
American writer

◆

Self-pity in its early stages is as snug as a feather mattress. Only when it hardens does it become uncomfortable.

MAYA ANGELOU (1928–)
African-American writer and poet

God made the world round so we would never be able to see too far down the road.

ISAK DINESEN (KAREN BLIXEN: 1885–1962)
Danish writer

◆

The great thing about getting older is that you don't lose all the other ages you've been.

MADELEINE L'ENGLE (1918–)
American writer

◆

Keep fit—but not for your men.
Do it for yourselves.

JANE FONDA (1937–)
American actress, political activist, and fitness advocate

It's a rather rude gesture, but at least it's clear what you mean.

KATHARINE HEPBURN (1909–)
(comment on spitting in the eye of director Joseph L. Mankiewicz)
American actress

◆

You would have thought I murdered someone, and perhaps I had, but only to give her successor a chance.

MARY PICKFORD (1893–1979)
(comment on the national furor when she bobbed her hair)
Canadian-American actress, writer, and philanthropist

◆

Nobody thinks it's silly to invest two hours' work in two minutes' enjoyment, but if cooking is evanescent, well, so is the ballet.

JULIA CHILD (1912–)
American chef, writer, and television personality

I know folks all have a tizzy about it, but I like a little bourbon of an evening. It helps me sleep. I don't much care what they say about it.

LILLIAN CARTER (1898–1983)
(comment on attitudes toward drinking in Plains, Georgia)
American nurse and Peace Corps worker, the mother of President Jimmy Carter

◆

Nobody can be exactly like me. Sometimes even I have trouble doing it.

TALLULAH BANKHEAD (1903–68)
American actress

◆

Toughness doesn't have to come in a pinstripe suit.

DIANNE FEINSTEIN (1933–)
(comment on being elected mayor of San Francisco)
American politician

On the whole, I haven't found men unduly loath to say, "I love you." The real trick is to get them to say, "Will you marry me?"

ILKA CHASE (1905–78)
American actress and writer

◆

The vote, I thought, means nothing to women. We should be *armed*.

EDNA O'BRIEN (1932–)
Irish writer

◆

I told her I would play a Venetian blind, dirt on the floor, anything.

WHOOPI GOLDBERG (1955–)
(remark concerning her letter to Alice Walker, in which she asked for a role in the movie version of Walker's book *The Color Purple*)
American actress and comic

I've been a woman for a little over 50 years and have gotten over my initial astonishment. As for conducting an orchestra, that's a job where I don't think sex plays much part.

NADIA BOULANGER (1887–1979)
(comment on becoming the first woman to conduct the Boston Symphony Orchestra)
American-French conductor

◆

Childbirth is more admirable than conquest, more amazing than self-defense, and as courageous as either one.

GLORIA STEINEM (1934–)
American feminist and writer

What you become is the price you paid to get what you used to want.

MIGNON MCLAUGHLIN (1915–)
American writer

◆

I praise loudly. I blame softly.

CATHERINE THE GREAT (CATHERINE II: 1729–96)
Russian empress from 1762 to 1796

◆

I have an inalienable, constitutional, and natural right to love whom I may, to love as long or as short a period as I can, to change that love every day if I please!

VICTORIA WOODHULL (1838–1937)
American feminist, writer, and editor

When I tell my kids that I married the first man I kissed, they just about throw up.

BARBARA BUSH (1925–)
American First Lady, the wife of President George Bush

◆

The poor wish to be rich, the rich wish to be happy, the single wish to be married, and the married wish to be dead.

ANN LANDERS (1918–)
American newspaper advice columnist

◆

A sobering thought: What if, right at this very moment, I *am* living up to my full potential?

JANE WAGNER (1935–)
American writer and humorist

There is time for work.
And time for love.
That leaves no other time.

COCO (GABRIELLE) CHANEL (1883–1971)
French fashion designer

◆

I am only one; but I am still one. I cannot do everything, but still I can do something. I will not refuse to do the something I can do.

HELEN KELLER (1880–1968)
American writer who was blind and deaf from birth

◆

The first duty of a human being is to assume the right relationship to society—more briefly, to find your real job and do it.

CHARLOTTE PERKINS GILMAN (1860–1935)
American poet, writer, and social critic

◆

Never doubt that a small group of thoughtful, committed citizens can change the world. Indeed, it is the only thing that ever has.

MARGARET MEAD (1901–78)
American anthropologist, curator, and writer

I don't want life to imitate art. I want life to *be* art.

CARRIE FISHER (1956–)
American actress and writer

◆

You can't get spoiled if you do your own ironing.

MERYL STREEP (1951–)
American actress

◆

We all live in suspense, from day to day, from hour to hour; in other words, we are the heroes of our own stories.

MARY MCCARTHY (1912–89)
American writer, critic, and editor

I am not eccentric. It's just that I am more alive than most people. I am an unpopular electric eel set in a pond of goldfish.

EDITH SITWELL (1887–1964)
English poet, editor, and critic known for, among other things, her unusual dress

◆

Call me madame.

FRANCES PERKINS (1882–1965)
(comment specifying the form of address she preferred as the first woman to hold a cabinet position in the United States)
American social worker and politician

If we had left it to the men *toilets* would have been the greatest obstacle to human progress. *Toilets* was always the reason women couldn't become engineers, or pilots, or even members of parliament. They didn't have women's toilets.

REBECCA WEST (1892–1983)
English writer

◆

Our struggle today is not to have a female Einstein get appointed as an assistant professor. It is for a woman schlemiel to get as quickly promoted as a male schlemiel.

BELLA ABZUG (1920–)
American politician

It's true that I never should have married, but I didn't want to live without a man. Brought up to respect the conventions, love had to end in marriage. I'm afraid it did.

BETTE DAVIS (1908–89)
American actress

◆

If you bungle raising your children, I don't think whatever else you do well matters very much.

JACQUELINE KENNEDY ONASSIS (1929–)
American editor and socialite

◆

In olden times sacrifices were made at the altar— a custom which is still continued.

HELEN ROWLAND (1876–1950)
American humorist and writer

The greater part of our happiness or misery depends on our dispositions and not our circumstances.

MARTHA WASHINGTON (1732–1802)
American First Lady, the wife of President George Washington

◆

If women can sleep their way to the top, how come they aren't there?

ELLEN GOODMAN (1941–)
American writer

◆

I shall be an autocrat; that's my trade. And the good Lord will forgive me; that's his.

CATHERINE THE GREAT (CATHERINE II: 1729–96)
Russian empress from 1762 to 1796

Fortunately, analysis is not the only way to resolve inner conflicts. Life itself remains a very effective therapist.

KAREN HORNEY (1885–1952)
American writer and lecturer

◆

I will make you shorter by a head.

ELIZABETH I (1533–1603)
(a favorite comment to those who opposed her wishes)
Queen of England from 1558 to 1603

◆

When men reach their sixties and retire, they go to pieces. Women just go right on cooking.

GAIL SHEEHY (1936–)
American writer and social critic

I finally figured out the only reason to be alive is to enjoy it.

RITA MAE BROWN (1944–)
American writer and poet

◆

It's matrimonial suicide to be jealous when you have a really good reason.

CLARE BOOTHE LUCE (1903–87)
American playwright, writer, politician, and diplomat

◆

If a man watches three football games in a row, he should be declared legally dead.

ERMA BOMBECK (1927–)
American writer and humorist

Positive reinforcement is hugging your husband when he does a load of laundry. Negative reinforcement is telling him he used too much detergent.

JOYCE BROTHERS (1925–)
American psychologist, writer, and television personality

◆

A girl can wait for the right man to come along but in the meantime she can have a wonderful time with all the wrong ones.

CHER (1946–)
American singer and actress

◆

If men can run the world, why can't they stop wearing neckties? How intelligent is it to start the day by tying a little noose around your neck?

LINDA ELLERBEE (1944–)
American writer and commentator

Dear, never forget one little point:
It's my business. You just work here.

ELIZABETH ARDEN (1884–1966)
(remark to her husband)
Canadian-American cosmetics tycoon

◆

If men had to have babies they would only ever
have one each.

DIANA, PRINCESS OF WALES (1961–)
English wife of Charles, Prince of Wales

◆

Plain women know more about men than
beautiful ones do.

KATHARINE HEPBURN (1909–)
American actress

Instead of comparing our lot with that of those who are more fortunate than we are, we should compare it with the lot of the great majority of our fellow men. It then appears that we are among the privileged.

HELEN KELLER (1880–1968)
American writer and lecturer who was blind and deaf from birth

◆

It is possible that blondes also prefer gentlemen.

MAMIE VAN DOREN (1933–)
American actress

◆

There are no dangerous thoughts; thinking itself is dangerous.

HANNAH ARENDT (1906–75)
German-American sociologist, historian, and philosopher

I do not weep at the world—
I am too busy sharpening my
oyster knife.

ZORA NEALE HURSTON (1903–60)
African-American writer

◆

We had taken the first step along the tortuous road that led to the sex war, sadomasochism, and ultimately to the whole contemporary snarl-up, to prostitution, prudery, Casanova, John Knox, Marie Stopes, white slavery, women's liberation, *Playboy* magazine, *crimes passionels,* censorship, strip clubs, alimony, pornography, and a dozen different brands of mania. This was the Fall. It had nothing to do with apples.

ELAINE MORGAN (1920–)
Welsh writer

◆

Never face facts; if you do you'll never get up in the morning.

MARLO THOMAS (1943–)
American actress

How it is possible that this absurd talk about a woman's sphere is still heard in the face of those millions of women who earn their bread by the sweat of their brows in field and factories, in streets and mines, behind the counter, and in the office?

HEDWIG DOHM (1833–1919)
German writer

◆

The only causes of regret are laziness, outbursts of temper, hurting others, prejudice, jealousy, and envy.

GERMAINE GREER (1939–)
Australian feminist and writer

There is perhaps one human being in a thousand who is passionately interested in his job for the job's sake. The difference is that if that one person in a thousand is a man, we say simply that he is passionately keen on his job; if she is a woman, we say she is a freak.

DOROTHY L. SAYERS (1893–1957)
English writer

◆

Dr. Kissinger was surprised that I knew where Ghana was.

SHIRLEY TEMPLE BLACK (1928–)
(remark on being appointed ambassador to Ghana)
American diplomat who was formerly a famous child actress

Winning may not be everything, but losing has little to recommend it.

DIANNE FEINSTEIN (1933–)
American politician

◆

Legislation and case law still exist in some parts of the United States permitting the "passion shooting" by a husband of a wife; the reverse, of course, is known as homicide.

DIANE B. SCHULDER (1937–)
American lawyer and educator

◆

Take your life in your own hands, and what happens? A terrible thing: no one to blame.

ERICA JONG (1943–)
American writer

Service is the rent you pay for being.

MARIAN WRIGHT EDELMAN (1937–)
African-American attorney and civil rights activist who founded the Children's Defense Fund

◆

Winning the prize wasn't half as exciting as doing the work itself.

MARIA GOEPPERT MAYER (1906–72)
German-American scientist who won the 1963 Nobel Prize for Physics

◆

Sometimes I worry about being a success in a mediocre world.

LILY TOMLIN (1936–)
American comic and actress

We must overcome the notion that we must be regular. It robs you of the chance to be extraordinary and leads you to the mediocre.

UTA HAGEN (1919–)
German-American actress and educator

◆

I spent fifteen years wandering about, weighed horribly with masses of paper and little else. Yet for this vocation of writing I was and am willing to die, and I consider very few other things of the slightest importance.

KATHERINE ANNE PORTER (1890–1980)
(remark concerning the long process of writing her novel *Ship of Fools*)
American writer

I am sure I read every book of fairy tales in our branch library, with one complaint—all that long golden hair. Never mind—my short brown hair became long and golden as I read and when I grew up I would write a book about a brown-haired girl to even things up.

BEVERLY CLEARY (1940–)
American writer

◆

Getting some brains in my head is more important than getting any so-called roses in my cheeks.

JEAN STAFFORD (1915–79)
(remark regarding her constant reading, made as a child in reply to the frequent parental injunction "You ought to be outdoors with the other youngsters getting roses in your cheeks.")
American writer

Ferdinand Marcos was the first male chauvinist to underestimate me.

CORAZON AQUINO (1933–)
Filipino politician who defeated Marcos to become the first female president of the Phillippine Islands

◆

Surrender to the maid sent hither, by God the King of Heaven, the keys of all the good towns you have taken and laid waste in France. And to you, King of England, if you do not thus, I am a chieftain of war and whenever I meet your followers in France, I will drive them out; if they will not obey, I will put them all to death.

JOAN OF ARC (1412–31)
(communiqué to Henry VI of England, whom she sought to drive out of Northern France in order to crown Charles VI King of France)
French patriot and saint burned at the stake as a heretic

As is the case in all branches of art, success depends in a very large measure upon individual initiative and exertion, and cannot be achieved except by dint of hard work.

ANNA PAVLOVA (1881–1931)
(comment regarding success as a dancer)
Russian ballerina

◆

Had God intended women only as a finer sort of cattle, He would not have made them reasonable. Brutes, a few degrees higher than monkeys, might have better fitted some men's lust, pride, and pleasure; especially those that desire to keep them ignorant to be tyrannized over.

BATHSUA MAKIN (1612–74)
English scholar and writer

Women who are content with light and easily broken ties do not act as I have done. They obtain what they desire and are still invited to dinner.

GEORGE ELIOT (MARY ANN EVANS: 1819–80)
English writer who was ostracized because she lived openly with the man she loved who, under nineteenth-century law, was unable to divorce his wife

◆

I know that I am a slave, and you are my lord. The law of this country has made you my master. You can bind my body, tie my hands, govern my actions; you are the strongest, and society adds to your power; but with my will, sir, you can do nothing.

GEORGE SAND (AURORE DUPIN DUDEVANT: 1804–76)
(from a letter to her husband)
French writer

If divorce has increased one thousand per cent, don't blame the woman's movement. Blame our obsolete sex roles, on which our marriages were based.

BETTY FRIEDAN (1921–)
American feminist and writer who founded the
National Organization for Women

◆

Life is too short to stuff a mushroom.

SHIRLEY CONRAN (1932–)
English designer and writer

◆

We will be ourselves and free, or die in the attempt. Harriet Tubman was not our great-grandmother for nothing.

ALICE WALKER (1944–)
American writer

Female size, especially brain size, has always been held to explain their unfitness for this or that; whole nineteenth-century theories were based on the smaller size of the brain of women and "inferior races"—until it was found that elephant's brains were even larger than men's.

KATHERINE WHITEHORN (1926–)
English writer

◆

Where divorce is allowed at all, society demands a specific grievance of one party against the other. The fact that the marriage may be a failure spiritually is seldom taken into account.

SUZANNE LAFOLLETTE (1893–1983)
American politician, writer, and feminist

Amazons live forever.

NEW YORK SUBWAY GRAFFITI, CIRCA 1982

◆

Book Orders

Additional copies of *Women Hold Up Half The Sky* may be ordered directly from the publisher.

❖ ❖ ❖

Please send me _____ copies of *Women Hold Up Half The Sky*. I enclose $9.95 ($7.95 plus $2.00 postage and handling) **per copy ordered**.

Name _____

Address _____

City_____ State_____ Zip _____

(Enclose your check or money order—no cash or C.O.D.'s, please.)

Price and availability are subject to change without notice. Please allow two to four weeks for delivery.

Mail your check and this order blank (or a photocopy) to: PLEASANT VIEW PRESS, P.O. Box 185, Pleasant View, TN 37146.